LIFE WITH
TYPE 1 DIABETES

BY CLARA MACCARALD

Published by The Child's World®
1980 Lookout Drive • Mankato, MN 56003-1705
800-599-READ • www.childsworld.com

Content Consultant: Elizabeth Littlejohn, M.D., M.S., Associate Professor of Pediatrics,
Michigan State University/Sparrow Medical Group

Photographs ©: iStockphoto, cover, 1, 12, 16; Shutterstock Images, 5, 8, 14, 18;
Jan Mika/Shutterstock Images, 6; Monkey Business Images/Shutterstock Images, 10;
Wave Break Media/Shutterstock Images, 20

ISBN 9781503825109
LCCN 2017959685

Printed in the United States of America
PA02375

TABLE OF
CONTENTS

FAST FACTS

- Type 1 diabetes is a disease in which a person's **immune system** destroys the beta cells in the pancreas. These cells make insulin. As a result, the person's pancreas makes very little or no insulin.

- Insulin is a **hormone**. It controls the amount of **glucose** in the bloodstream. Cells turn glucose into energy the body needs to work properly.

- Approximately 1.3 million people in the United States have type 1 diabetes. People with type 1 diabetes monitor their blood glucose levels and give themselves insulin throughout the day to keep blood glucose levels as normal as possible.

- Food affects blood glucose levels. People with type 1 diabetes count the amount of **carbohydrates** in the food they eat to better manage their glucose levels.

- Scientists aren't exactly sure what causes type 1 diabetes. It is likely caused by a combination of a person's **genes** and something in the environment, such as a **virus**.

- There is no cure for type 1 diabetes. Taking insulin, monitoring blood glucose, exercising regularly, and eating well are the best ways to manage type 1 diabetes.

GLUCOSE AND THE DIGESTIVE SYSTEM

In the digestive system, the stomach breaks food down into glucose. The liver stores some glucose for the body to use later. The small intestine absorbs glucose, which then enters the bloodstream. Insulin made by the pancreas controls the amount of glucose in the bloodstream.

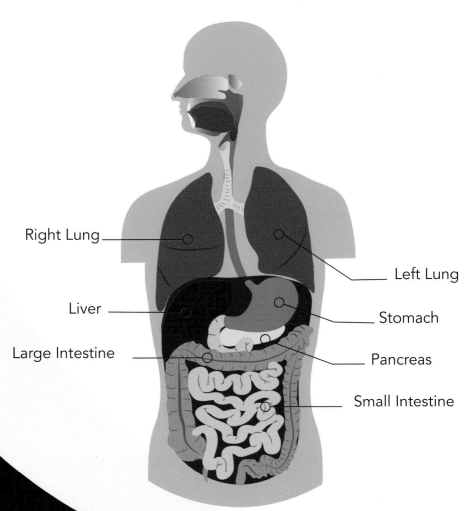

Right Lung

Left Lung

Liver

Stomach

Large Intestine

Pancreas

Small Intestine

Chapter 1

SCOTT'S NEW LIFE

Eleven-year-old Scott fell onto the couch after soccer practice. He was exhausted! He hadn't been feeling well for many weeks. He was always tired and continually thirsty. He also couldn't focus as well as he used to. Although he was eating three meals a day, he was losing weight. His mother decided it was time to visit the family doctor. She helped Scott into the car and drove him to the doctor's office.

Scott first saw a nurse at the doctor's office. The nurse explained to Scott that she had to check his blood glucose level. She poked the tip of his finger to get a drop of blood. She put the drop of blood on a strip. Then the nurse fed the strip into a blood glucose meter.

◀ **Extreme exhaustion can be a sign of high blood sugar.**

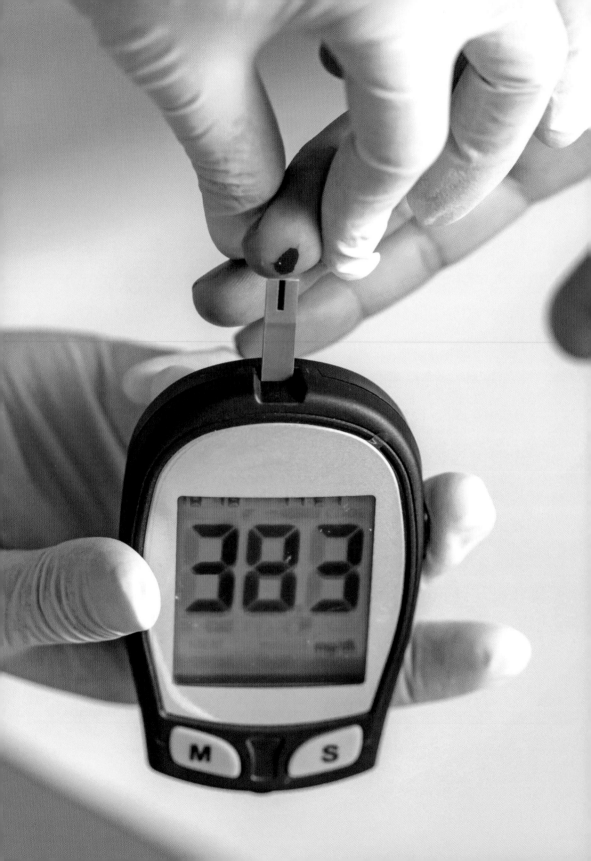

The meter showed that Scott had too much glucose, or sugar, in his blood. The doctor explained that Scott's body wasn't making the insulin it needed to control the glucose in his blood. This meant that Scott had type 1 diabetes.

Scott learned that he would have to take daily insulin injections to replace the insulin his body no longer made. The injections would help him manage his diabetes.

CHECKING GLUCOSE

Many people with type 1 diabetes test their blood glucose, or blood sugar, by using a blood glucose meter. Other people use a continuous glucose monitor. Part of this monitor stays under the skin and sends a signal to a handheld device, which displays a person's current glucose level. A continuous glucose monitor can also sound an alarm when blood sugars rise too high or drop too low.

◄ **A blood glucose meter measures a person's glucose levels.**

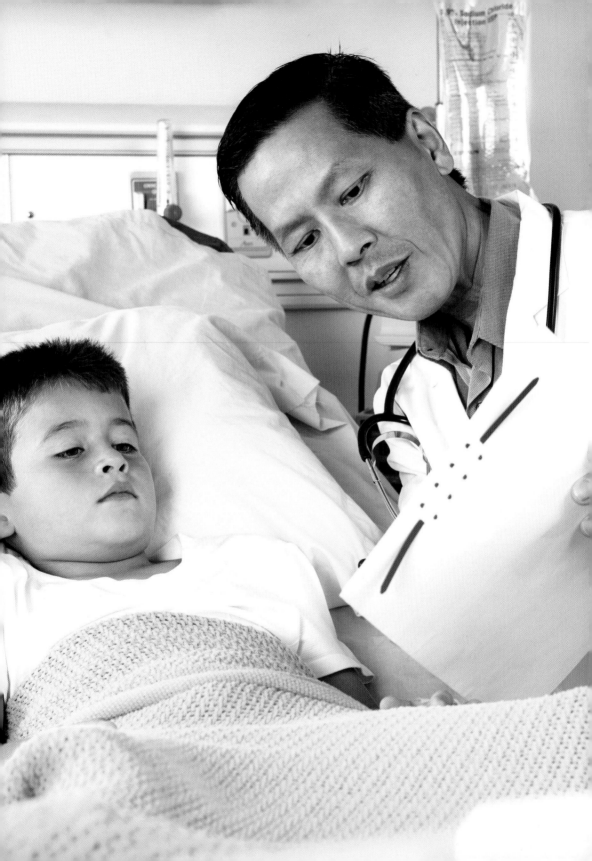

Scott would also have to monitor his blood sugar levels and count the carbohydrates he ate throughout the day.

A medical team made up of doctors, nurses, and dieticians would help Scott manage his diabetes. Nurse educators would teach Scott and his parents about Scott's diabetes. They would also keep the other nurses on Scott's team updated on Scott's treatment plan. Scott's treatment plan would help him keep track of his diet, exercise, glucose levels, and insulin.

Scott's doctor assured him that he could continue to live an active and healthy life. The nurse gave Scott his first shot of insulin in his belly. A little while later, he began to feel better.

Scott knew he would have to work hard to stay healthy. But he would have a lot of help. Scott and his family were ready to take on this challenge.

◄ **A medical team helps someone with type 1 diabetes figure out a treatment plan.**

Chapter 2

HOLLY'S APPOINTMENT

Ten-year-old Holly watched the traffic outside the car window as her dad drove. She was on her way to visit a special doctor called an **endocrinologist**. Because of her type 1 diabetes, her doctor needed to check her health every three months.

Once at the doctor's office, Holly's dad handed her health logs and blood glucose meter to the medical assistant. The health logs were daily records of all the food Holly had eaten, her insulin doses, and her glucose readings. These records would help the doctor determine whether Holly's treatment plan was working or whether it needed to be changed.

◀ People with type 1 diabetes have checkups with a doctor every few months.

13

▲ **An insulin pump gives a person regular doses of insulin throughout the day.**

When a nurse called her name, Holly and her dad followed the nurse into a room. The nurse pricked Holly's finger to do a blood test. Holly was used to the slight pinch from checking her own glucose.

The doctor then went over Holly's health logs and the results of her blood tests. Holly was doing a good job keeping health logs and managing her diabetes. The doctor suggested considering an insulin pump.

The pump would **infuse** insulin into Holly's body through a tube. This would help her manage her glucose levels.

After her checkup, Holly and her dad went to a restaurant for lunch. Holly made sure to inject her insulin shot after counting the amount of carbohydrates she would eat during the meal.

Holly would have another appointment with her doctor in a few months. But for now, her long day was over.

CARBOHYDRATE COUNTING

Carbohydrates are found in many types of foods. Foods that are high in carbohydrates include bread, potatoes, and pasta. People with type 1 diabetes work with a medical team to determine proper insulin-to-carbohydrate ratio. This ratio is the amount of insulin needed to balance the intake of carbohydrates. Knowing the proper ratio helps a person with type 1 diabetes maintain more stable blood sugar levels.

Chapter 3

WILLA'S DAY AT THE PARK

Eleven-year-old Willa bounded into the kitchen. Her parents were making breakfast. Her stomach grumbled. But she couldn't eat yet. First, she needed to check her blood sugar. She read her blood glucose level off her continuous glucose monitor.

Willa's glucose levels had been higher than usual last night. Her mom had programmed her insulin pump to deliver additional insulin, which brought her glucose levels down. But this morning, her glucose levels were still slightly above normal.

◀ Foods with carbohydrates can increase glucose levels.

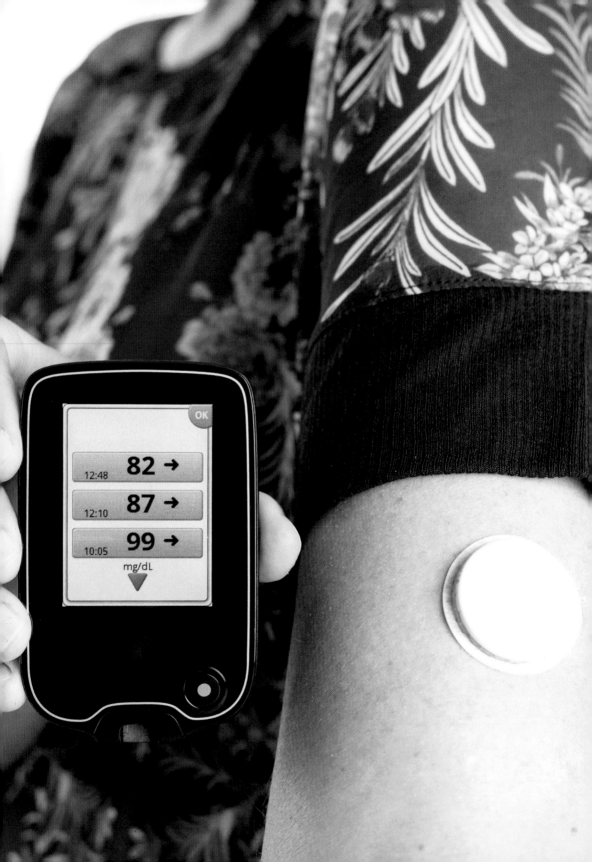

Willa's mom entered Willa's blood glucose level into her insulin pump. Willa read the amount of carbohydrates per serving off of a package of whole grain bagels. Willa's mom also entered the amount of carbohydrates Willa would eat for breakfast into the insulin pump. Based on these numbers, the pump calculated the dose of insulin Willa would need.

◄ **People with type 1 diabetes can use a continuous glucose monitor to check their glucose levels.**

TYPE 2 DIABETES

When someone has type 1 diabetes, his or her pancreas produces little or no insulin. Type 2 diabetes occurs when the pancreas produces insulin, but the body can't use the insulin properly. A person's genes can cause type 2 diabetes, and it can also be caused by extra body weight or lack of exercise. Some people with type 2 diabetes can treat themselves by changing their diet or becoming more active. But others must also take medication or inject insulin. Type 2 diabetes is more common than type 1 diabetes.

▲ **People with type 1 diabetes can have healthy and active lives.**

Later that day, Willa and her family went to a park. Willa snacked on nuts. After a while, sweat beaded on her forehead. She felt dizzy. Her vision blurred. The monitor on her arm buzzed. It was warning her that her glucose levels were low.

Willa sat on the trail. She breathed deeply to stay calm. She realized that the insulin calculations might have been a bit off that morning, so she got more insulin than she needed.

Willa's mom knew what to do. She gave Willa candies and a juice box. She temporarily lowered Willa's insulin infusion through Willa's pump. After a little while, Willa felt better. Her glucose levels had risen. They started on the trail again.

THINK ABOUT IT

- How is the everyday life of a person with type 1 diabetes different from the life of a person without it?
- If you had type 1 diabetes, would you want to use an insulin pump? Why or why not?
- How could you help a friend with type 1 diabetes?

GLOSSARY

carbohydrates (kar-boh-HYE-drayts): Carbohydrates are parts of food that give the body energy. People with type 1 diabetes must consider how many carbohydrates they will eat at a meal.

endocrinologist (en-doh-kri-NAHL-oh-jist): An endocrinologist is a doctor who treats hormone-related conditions. Someone who has type 1 diabetes visits an endocrinologist every few months.

genes (JEENZ): Genes are located within the body's cells, and they determine which traits are passed down to a child from parents. Genes can influence whether a person has diabetes.

glucose (GLOO-kose): Glucose is a type of sugar made from food, which cells use for energy. People with type 1 diabetes must check their glucose levels every day.

hormone (HOR-mohn): A hormone is a chemical that affects the way a person's body functions or develops. Insulin is an important hormone.

immune system (i-MYOON SISS-tuhm): The immune system is the part of a person's body that fights against infections and diseases. When someone has type 1 diabetes, the person's immune system destroys beta cells in the pancreas.

infuse (in-FYUSE): To infuse is to deliver doses of a medicine underneath the skin. Insulin pumps infuse insulin into the body of someone with type 1 diabetes.

virus (VY-ruhss): A virus is an organism that can cause a disease. A virus may cause a person's immune system to attack beta cells in the pancreas, which leads to type 1 diabetes.

TO LEARN MORE

Books

Bryan, Jenny. *I Have Diabetes.* New York, NY: Gareth Stevens, 2011.

Edge, Julie. *Can I Tell You about Diabetes (Type 1)? A Guide for Friends, Family and Professionals.* Philadelphia, PA: Jessica Kingsley, 2014.

Silverstein, Alvin, Virginia Silverstein, and Laura Silverstein Nunn. *Handy Health Guide to Diabetes.* Berkeley Heights, NJ: Enslow, 2014.

Web Sites

Visit our Web site for links about type 1 diabetes:
childsworld.com/links

Note to Parents, Teachers, and Librarians: We routinely verify our Web links to make sure they are safe and active sites. So encourage your readers to check them out!

SELECTED BIBLIOGRAPHY

Chase, H. Peter, and David M. Maahs. *A First Book for Understanding Diabetes.* Denver, CO: Children's Diabetes Foundation, 2014.

Gregg, Jennifer, Glenn Callaghan, and Steven Hayes. *Diabetes Lifestyle Book: Facing Your Fears & Making Changes for a Long and Healthy Life.* Oakland, CA: New Harbinger Publications, 2007.

Kaufman, Francine R., and Emily Westfall. *Insulin Pumps and Continuous Glucose Monitoring: A User's Guide to Effective Diabetes Management.* Arlington, VA: American Diabetes Association, 2017.

Milchovich, Sue K., and Barbara Dunn-Long. *Diabetes Mellitus: A Practical Handbook.* Eau Claire, WI: Bull Publishing Company, 2015.

"Type 1 Diabetes." *American Diabetes Association.* American Diabetes Association, n.d. Web. 20 Oct. 2017.

INDEX

ABOUT THE AUTHOR

Clara MacCarald is a freelance writer with a master's degree in biology. She lives with her family in an off-grid house nestled in the forests of central New York. When not parenting her daughter, she spends her time writing nonfiction books for kids.